Commercial Law:
Diagrams for Law Students
VisuaLaw Study Guide Volume 10

Markus McDowell

SULIS
ACADEMIC
PRESS

An imprint of Sulis Internatuonal
Los Angeles | London

This VisuaLaw Study Guide diagrams are based on the University of London Study Guide for Commercial Law. This publication is an independent work, and is not connected with nor endorsed by the University.

Published by Sulis Academic Press
An imprint of Sulis International
www.sulisinternational.com

COMMERCIAL LAW

ISBN-13: 978-1530233380
ISBN-10: 1530233380

First Edition: February 2016
Second Printing: February 2018

1. Law   2. Commercial   3. General

CONTENTS

PREFACE

Welcome to *Commercial Law: Diagrams for Law Students*. **Diagrams** contain flow charts, diagrams, and other visual aids for each topic in the study of UK Commercial Law.

We suggest that, as you read, you use colored highlighters to high certain information. Colors aid in memorization and recognition. Our suggestions:

> Red: important legal terms
> Green: common law cases
> Blue: statutes
> Purple: EU cases or statutes

These Study Guides are not intended as a substitute for required readings or any other assignments. Everything you need to know to pass the exams is not included here—this book is an outline of the subject and a companion study tool. If you understand and can discuss each element on each page, you will be well on your way to understanding the subject.

Send questions, errata, and suggestions to academic@sulisinternational.com. Your input will help us continue to update and refine these study guides.

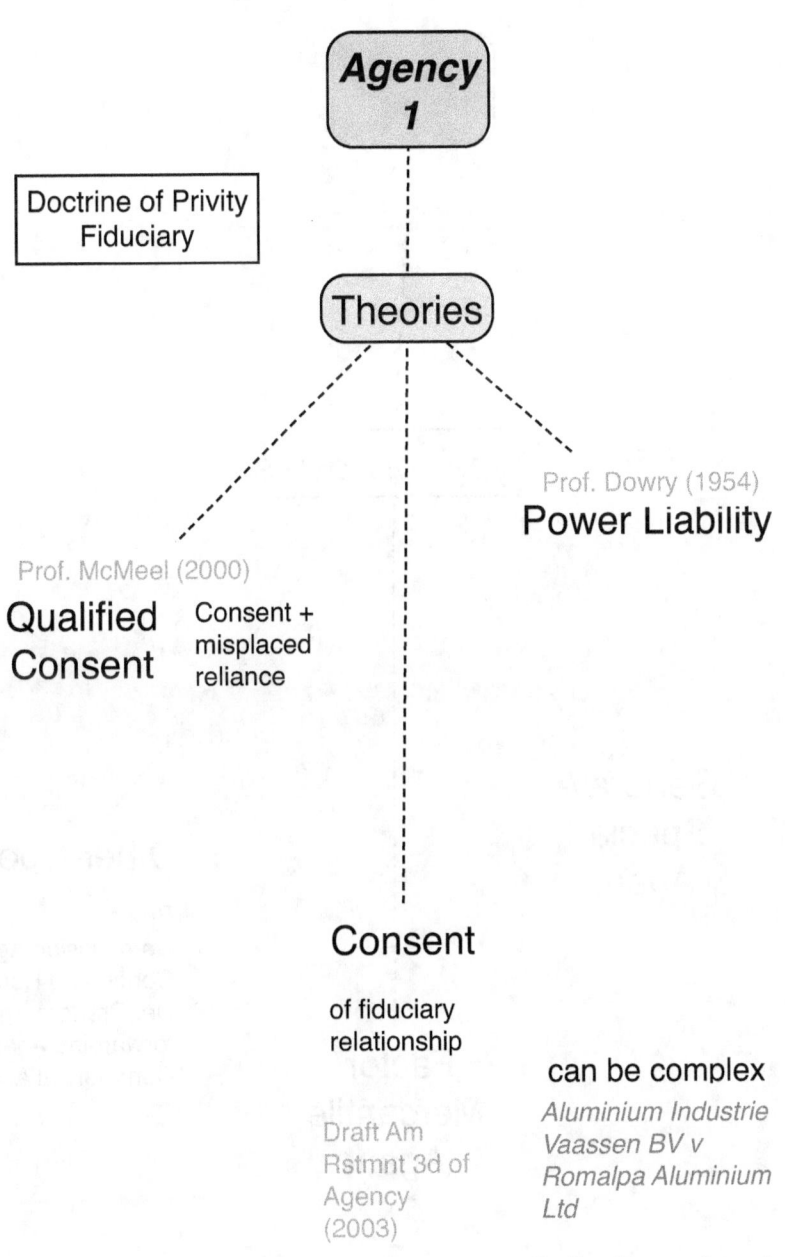

Agency 1

Doctrine of Privity
Fiduciary

Theories

Prof. Dowry (1954)
Power Liability

Prof. McMeel (2000)
Qualified Consent — Consent + misplaced reliance

Consent

of fiduciary
relationship

Draft Am
Rstmnt 3d of
Agency
(2003)

can be complex

*Aluminium Industrie
Vaassen BV v
Romalpa Aluminium
Ltd*

distinctions of an A

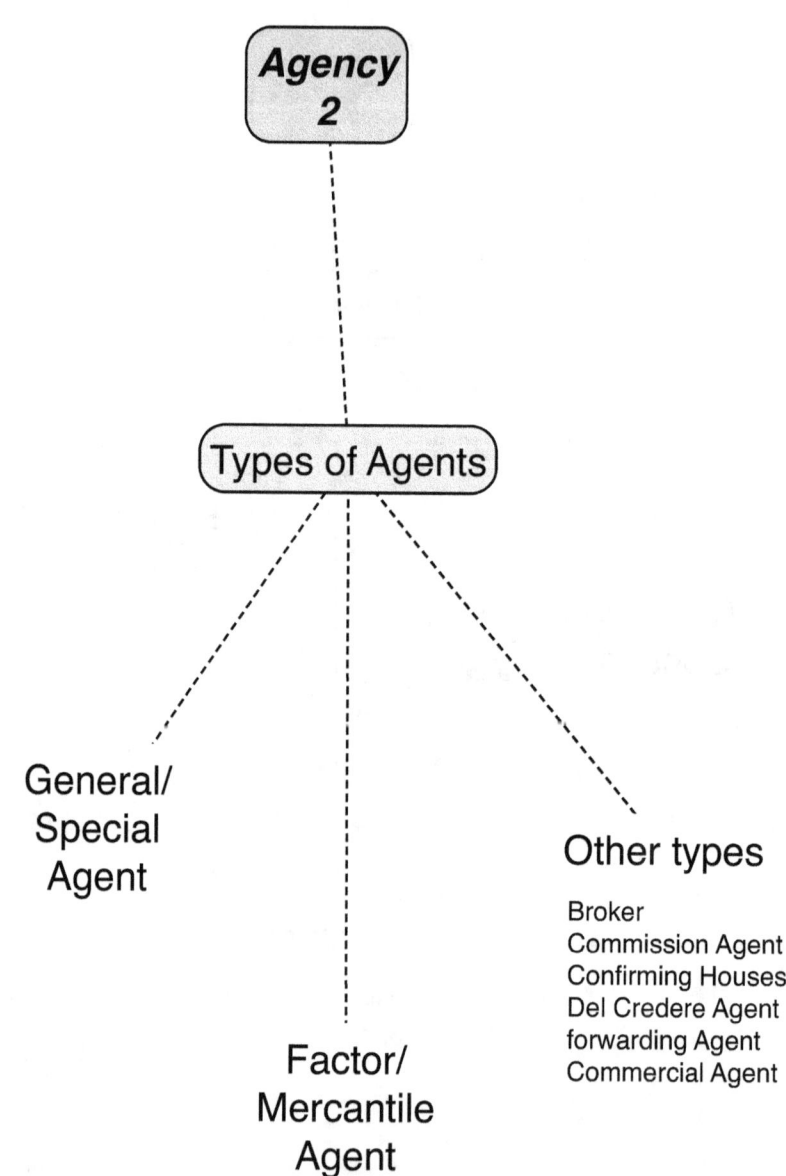

Agency 2

Types of Agents

General/ Special Agent

Factor/ Mercantile Agent

Other types

Broker
Commission Agent
Confirming Houses
Del Credere Agent
forwarding Agent
Commercial Agent

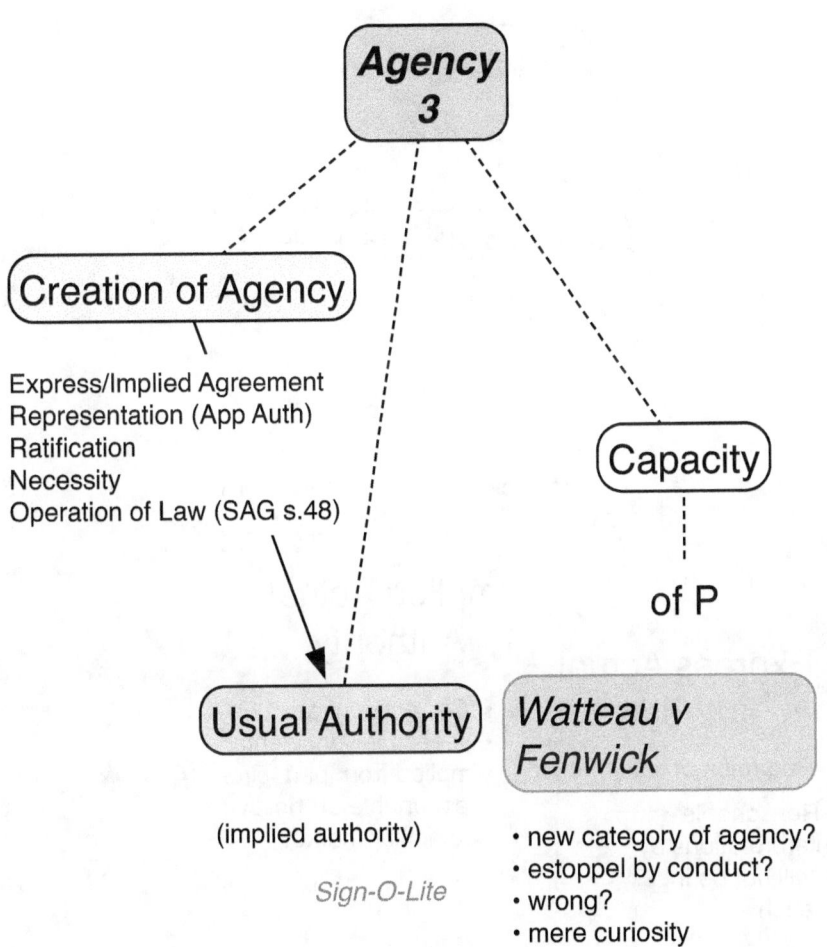

Agency 3

Creation of Agency

Express/Implied Agreement
Representation (App Auth)
Ratification
Necessity
Operation of Law (SAG s.48)

Capacity

of P

Usual Authority

(implied authority)

Sign-O-Lite

Watteau v Fenwick

• new category of agency?
• estoppel by conduct?
• wrong?
• mere curiosity

4

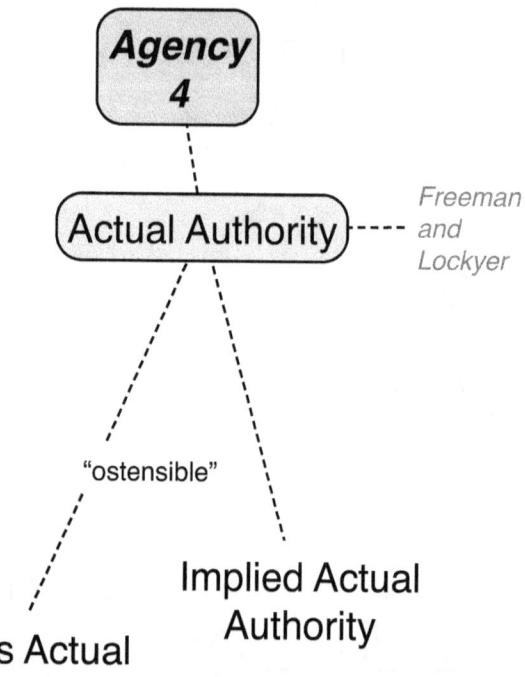

Agency 4

Actual Authority ---- *Freeman and Lockyer*

"ostensible"

Express Actual Authority

• Reg rules of construction

• Reasonable interpretations by A will not be in breach

Ireland v Livingston

European Asian Bank AG v Punjab & Sind Bank No. 2

Implied Actual Authority

• (Cannot contradict EAA)
• Necessarily incidental
• implied from part. circ.
• reasonable 3P believe
• particular market

Hely-Hutchison

Smith v Butler [2012]

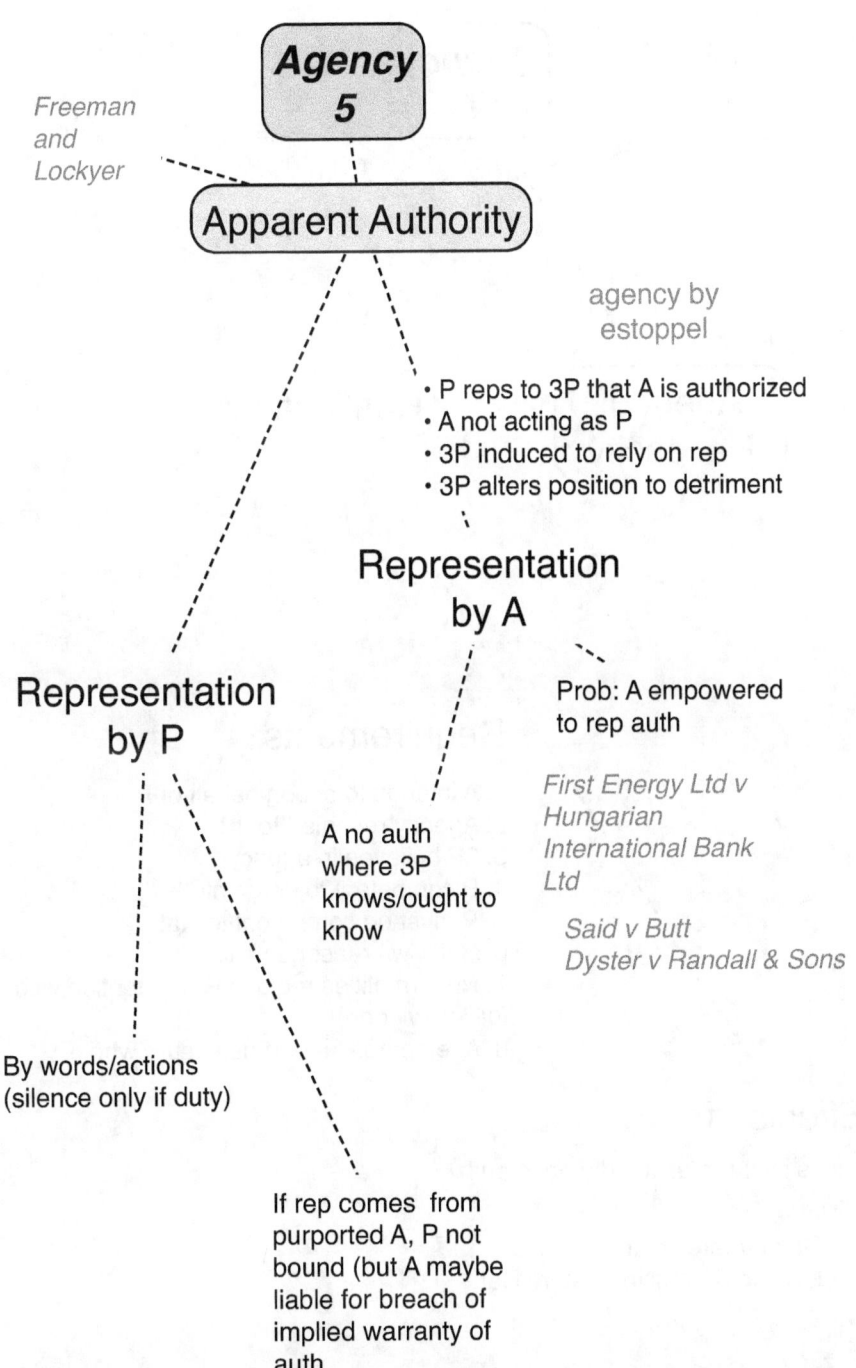

Agency
5

*Freeman
and
Lockyer*

Apparent Authority

agency by
estoppel

• P reps to 3P that A is authorized
• A not acting as P
• 3P induced to rely on rep
• 3P alters position to detriment

Representation
by A

Representation
by P

Prob: A empowered
to rep auth

*First Energy Ltd v
Hungarian
International Bank
Ltd*

*Said v Butt
Dyster v Randall & Sons*

A no auth
where 3P
knows/ought to
know

By words/actions
(silence only if duty)

If rep comes from
purported A, P not
bound (but A maybe
liable for breach of
implied warranty of
auth

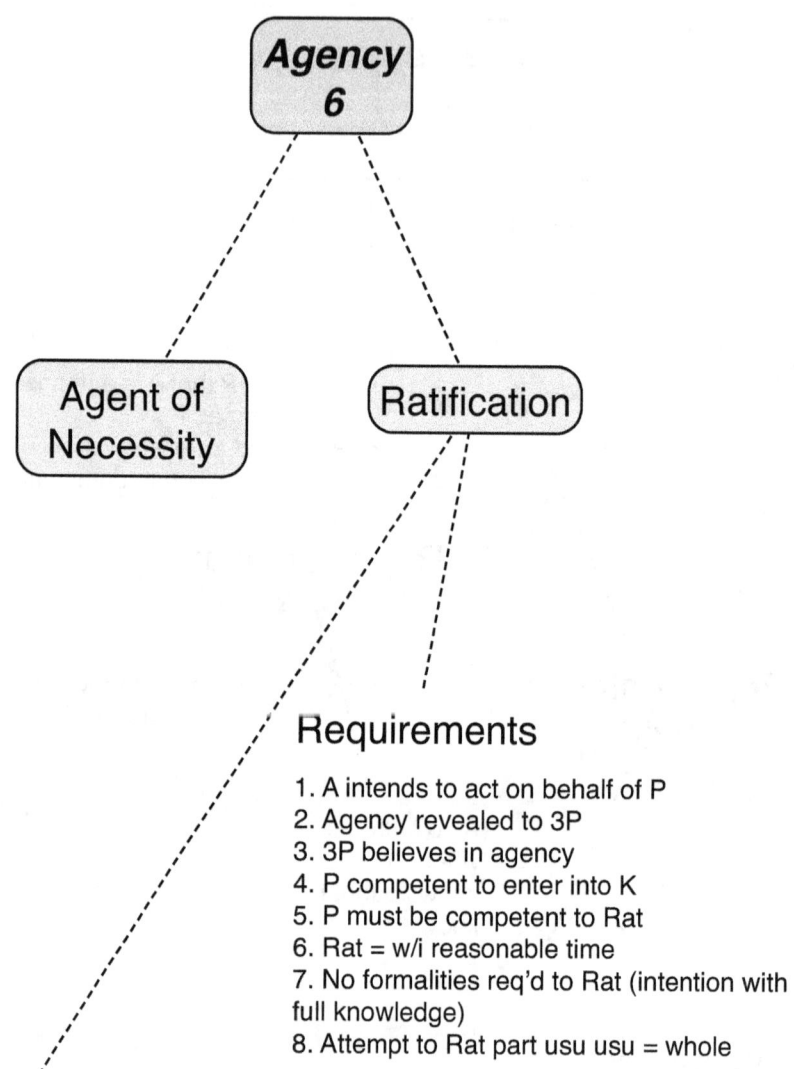

**Agency
6**

**Agent of
Necessity**

Ratification

Requirements

1. A intends to act on behalf of P
2. Agency revealed to 3P
3. 3P believes in agency
4. P competent to enter into K
5. P must be competent to Rat
6. Rat = w/i reasonable time
7. No formalities req'd to Rat (intention with full knowledge)
8. Attempt to Rat part usu usu = whole

Effects of

Places all three as if A did have auth

Unless:
- Other interests unfair; void.   *Brown v Bird*
- If A and 3P rescind before Rat.   *Walter James*

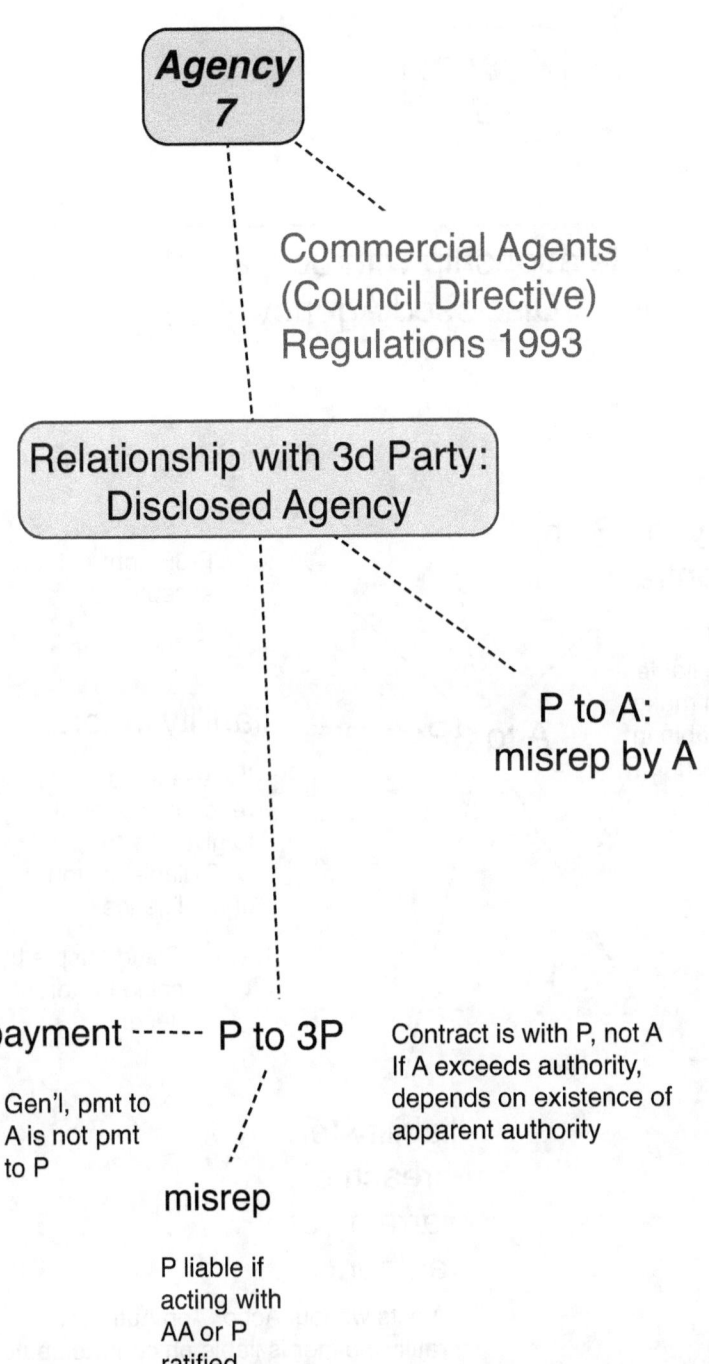

Agency 7

Commercial Agents
(Council Directive)
Regulations 1993

Relationship with 3d Party:
Disclosed Agency

P to A:
misrep by A

payment ------ P to 3P   Contract is with P, not A
                                If A exceeds authority,
Gen'l, pmt to   depends on existence of
A is not pmt   apparent authority
to P

misrep

P liable if
acting with
AA or P
ratified

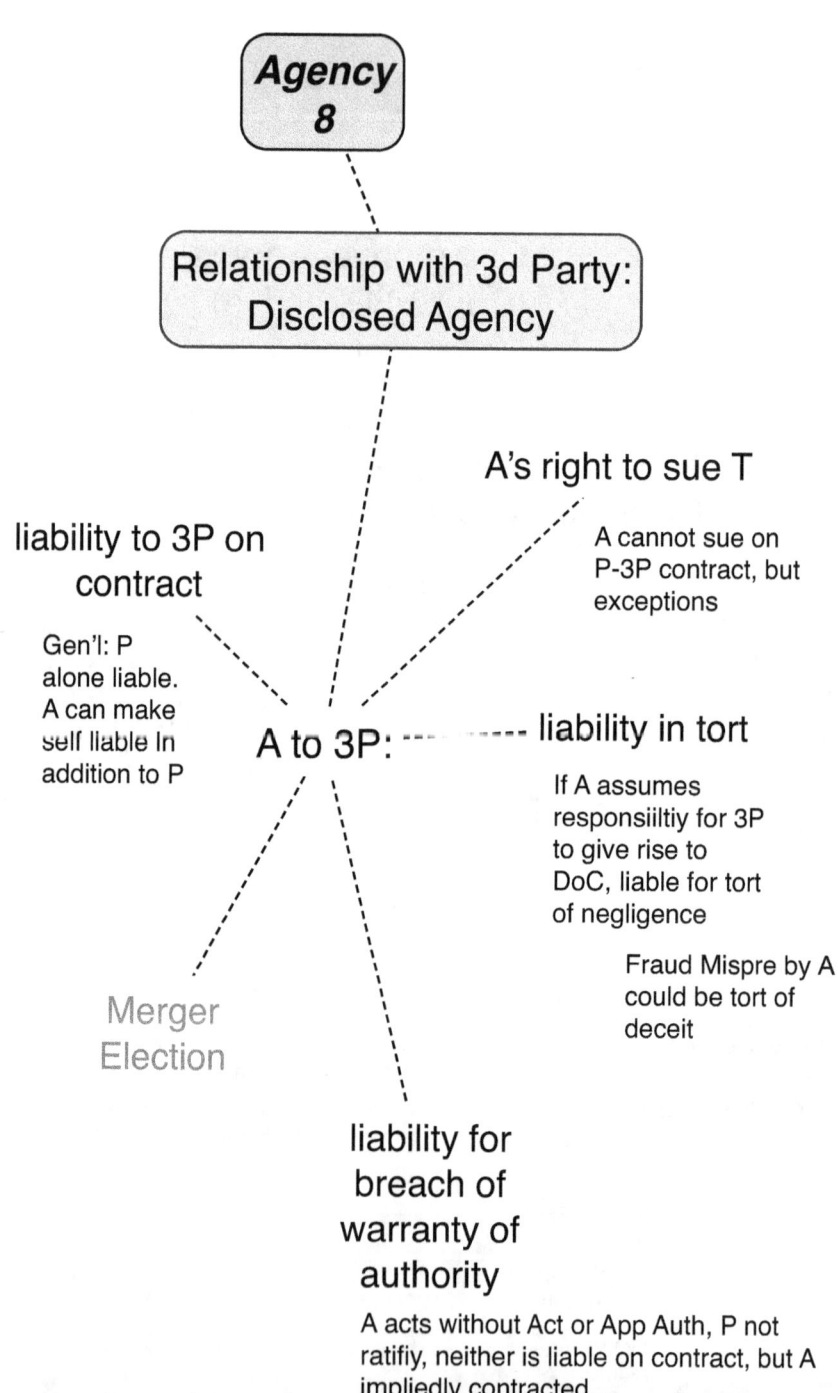

Agency 8

Relationship with 3d Party: Disclosed Agency

A to 3P:

liability to 3P on contract

Gen'l: P alone liable. A can make self liable In addition to P

A's right to sue T

A cannot sue on P-3P contract, but exceptions

liability in tort

If A assumes responsiiltiy for 3P to give rise to DoC, liable for tort of negligence

Fraud Mispre by A could be tort of deceit

Merger Election

liability for breach of warranty of authority

A acts without Act or App Auth, P not ratifiy, neither is liable on contract, but A impliedly contracted.

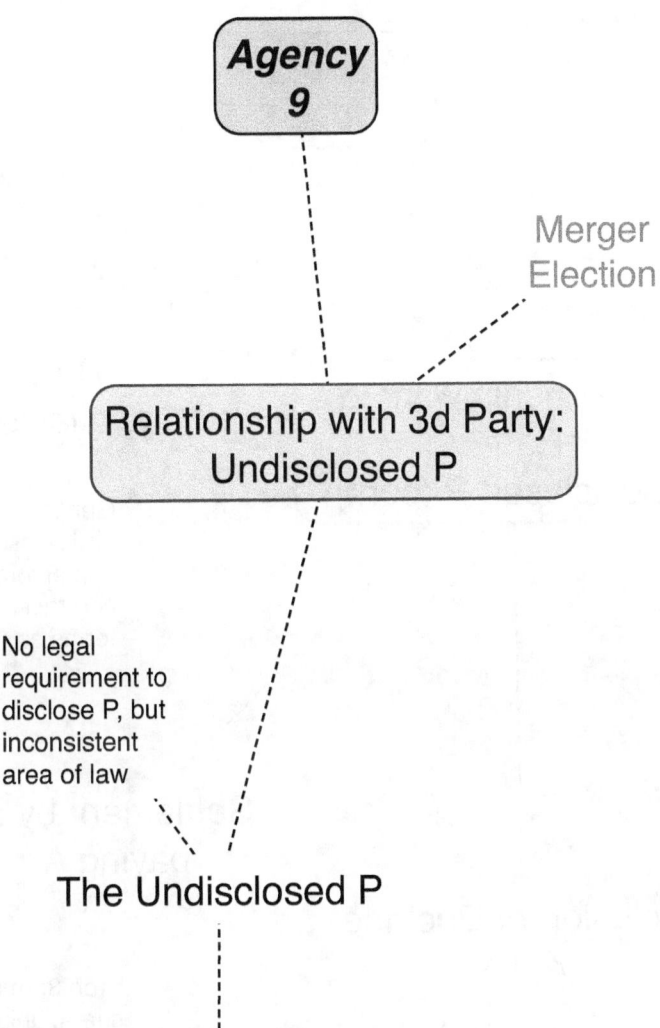

Agency 9

Merger
Election

Relationship with 3d Party:
Undisclosed P

No legal
requirement to
disclose P, but
inconsistent
area of law

The Undisclosed P

Contract is b/t A and 3P until 3p discovers

When 3P discovers. can choose to sue P or A
before 3P discovers, P may intervene to enforce contract

If A acts w/o authority, P cannot
sue, ratification not possible

Unidentified and undisclosed are different

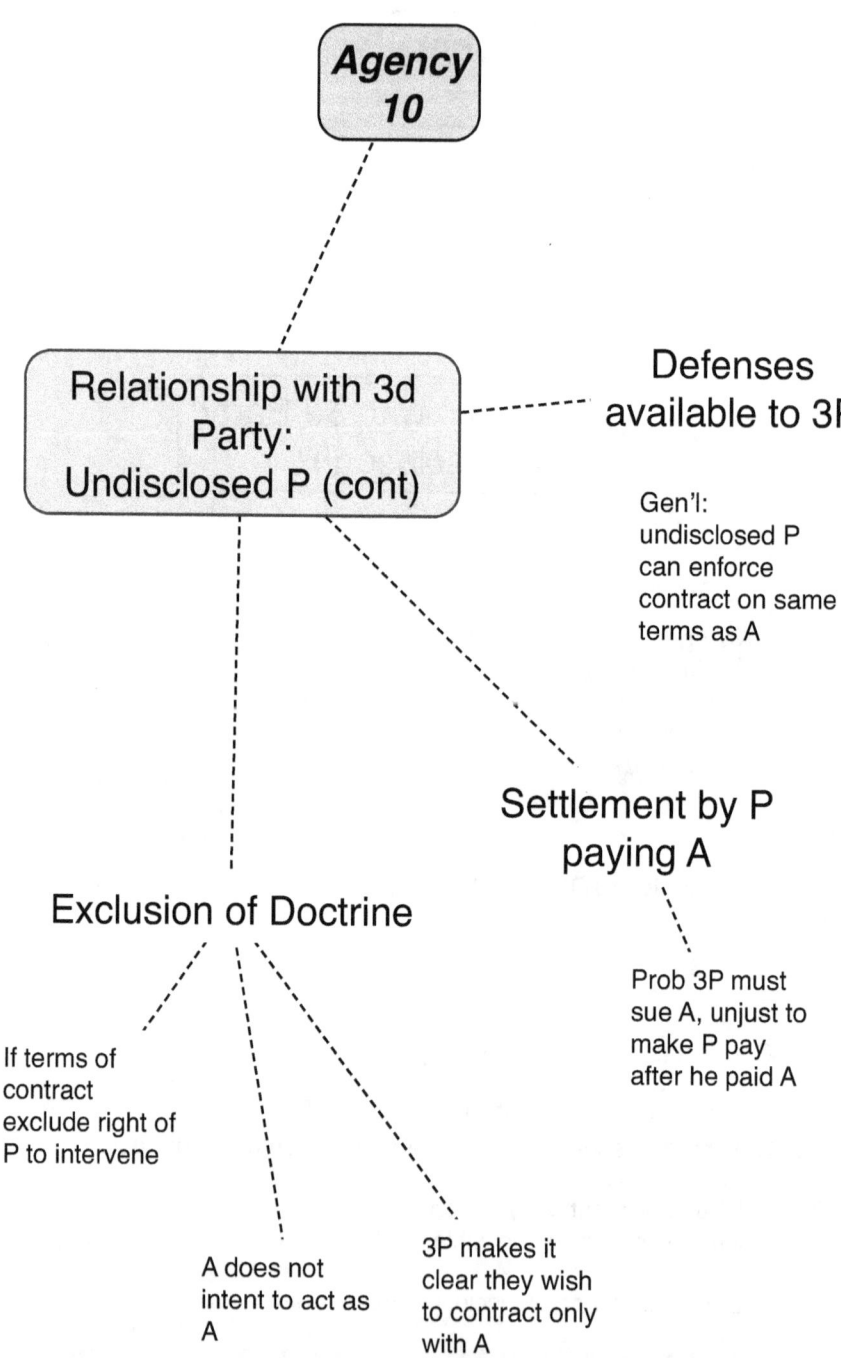

Agency 10

Relationship with 3d Party:
Undisclosed P (cont)

Defenses available to 3P

Gen'l: undisclosed P can enforce contract on same terms as A

Settlement by P paying A

Prob 3P must sue A, unjust to make P pay after he paid A

Exclusion of Doctrine

If terms of contract exclude right of P to intervene

A does not intent to act as A

3P makes it clear they wish to contract only with A

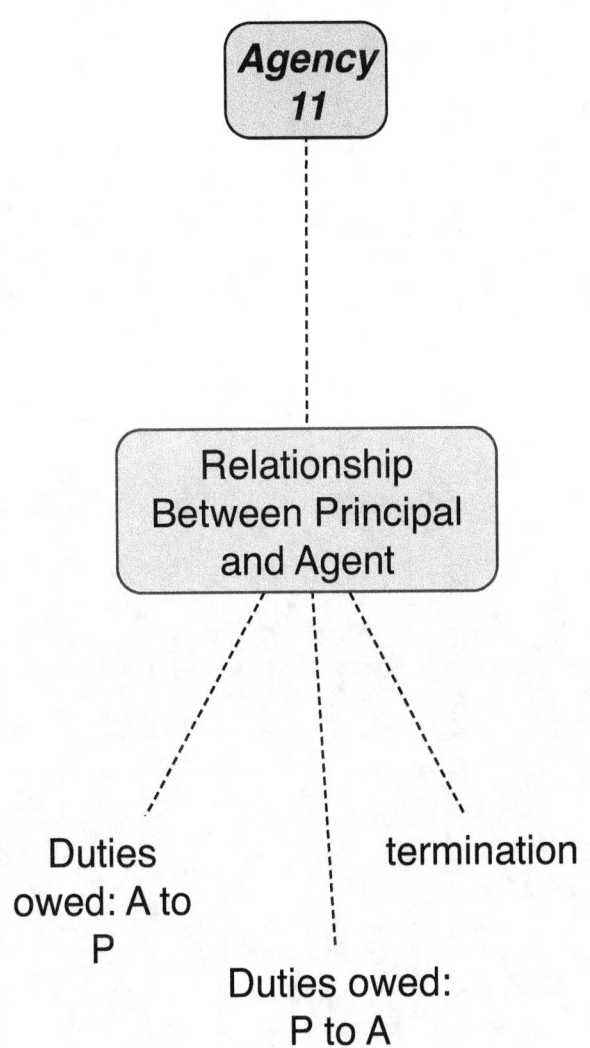

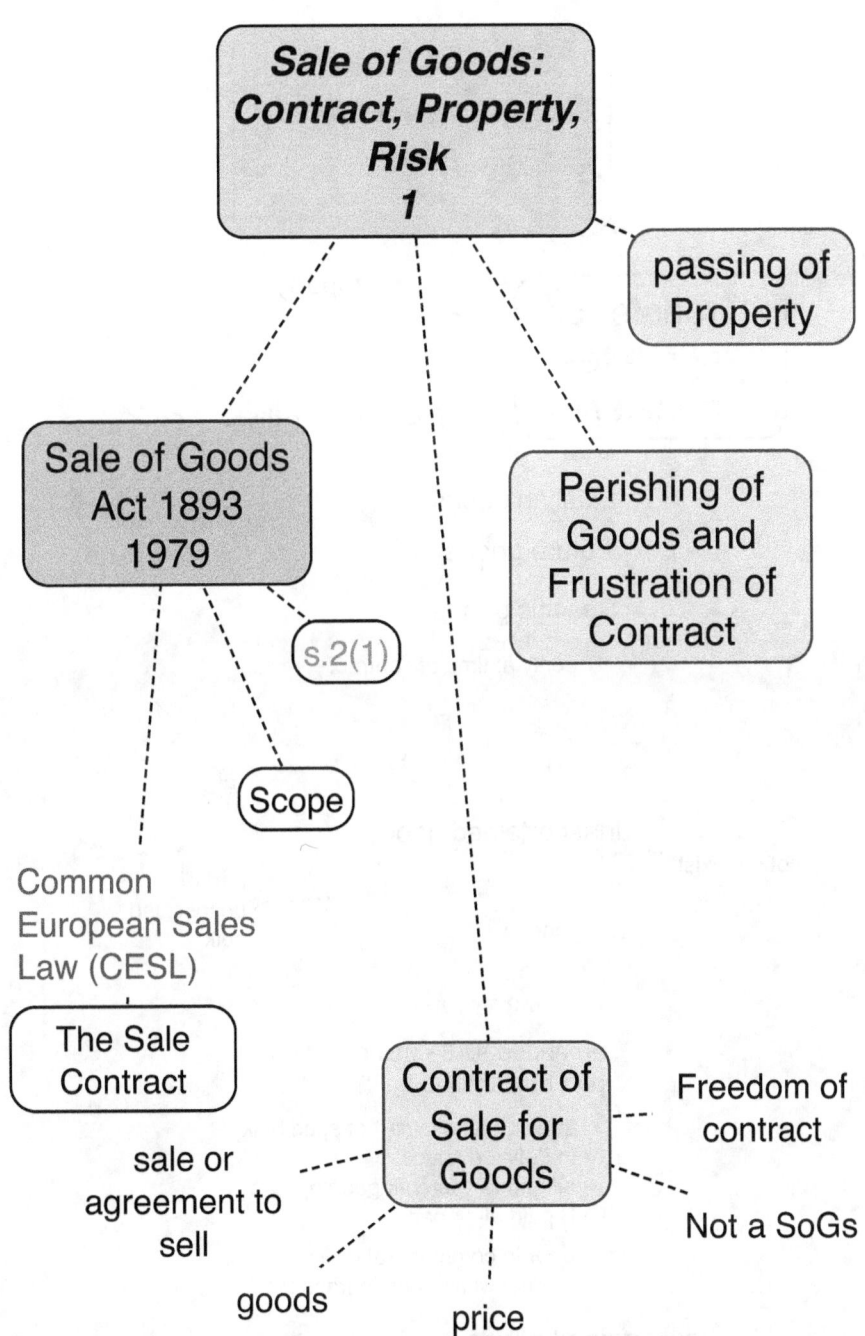

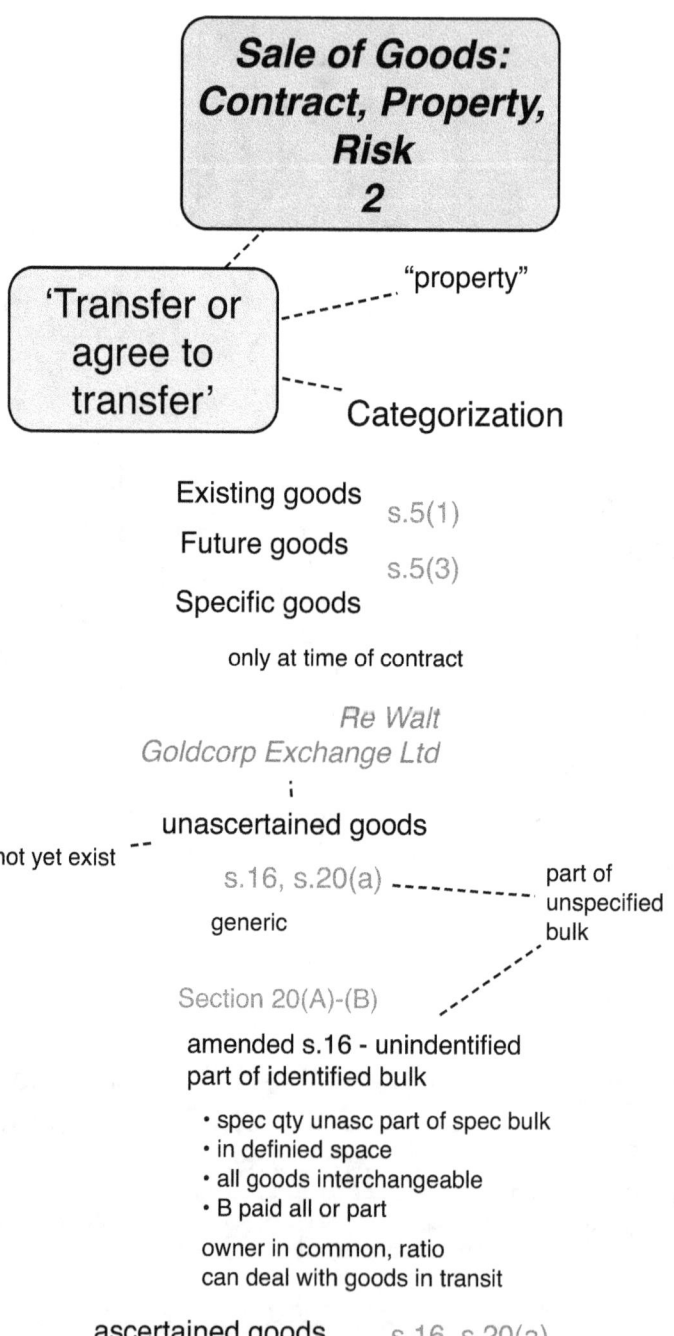

Sale of Goods: Contract, Property, Risk

2

'Transfer or agree to transfer'

"property"

Categorization

Existing goods   s.5(1)

Future goods

   s.5(3)

Specific goods

only at time of contract

Re Walt Goldcorp Exchange Ltd

unascertained goods

not yet exist

s.16, s.20(a)

generic

part of unspecified bulk

Section 20(A)-(B)

amended s.16 - unindentified part of identified bulk

- spec qty unasc part of spec bulk
- in definied space
- all goods interchangeable
- B paid all or part

owner in common, ratio can deal with goods in transit

ascertained goods   s.16, s.20(a)

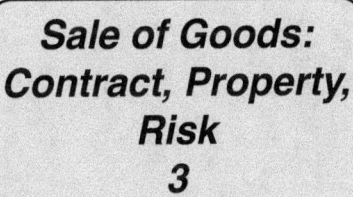

Sale of Goods: Contract, Property, Risk 3

'Transfer or agree to transfer' (cont) ----- Key Principles

Property/possession distinct

Only when ascertained   *Tarling v Baxter*

When intended

s.17

s.18   No intention?

No eq int   *Re Wait*

Rule 1   sp. goods in deliverable state

Dennant v Skinner

Rule 2   sp. goods in deliverable state by B

Rule 3   *Underwood v Burgh Castle*

Rule 4   sp. goods price to be ascertained by seller

but see   *Nanka-Bruce v Commonwealth Trust*

Rule 5

on approval, sale, or return (a bailee, no contract of SoG yet)

Poole v Smith's Car Sales

unascertained goods & 'unconditionally appropriated to the contract

Kulkarni v Manor Credit (Davenham) Ltd [2010]

5(3)–(4)

ascertainment by exhaustion   *The Elafi*

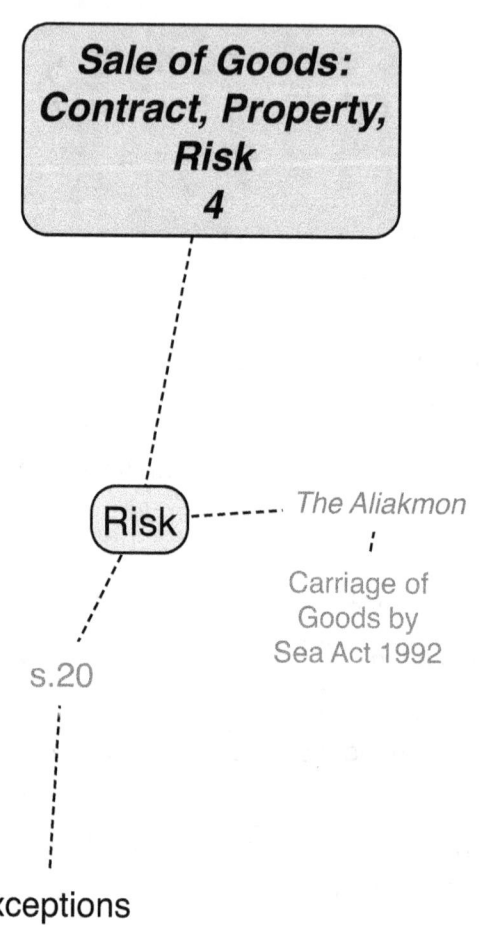

Sale of Goods: Contract, Property, Risk

4

Risk ------- *The Aliakmon*

Carriage of Goods by Sea Act 1992

s.20

Exceptions

Agreement *Head v Tattersall; Sterns v Vickers Ltd*
s.20(1)

Party fault   s.20(2)

Bailee lack of RC   s.20(3)

s.32
S req'd to send

Sale of Goods: Contract, Property, Risk

5

Transfer of Title

s.21(1) --- nemo dat quod non habet

Bishopsgate Motor Finance Corporation

Exceptions   *National Employer's Mutual General Insurance Assocn Ltd v Jones*

Estoppel

s.21(1)   *Henderson & Co v Williams*

Sale under voidable title   s.23

Car and Universal Finance Co Ltd v Caldwell
Newtons of Wembley Ltd v Williams

S in possession; property passed; B sells to C (GF NN)

Michael Gerson   s.24; s.8 Factors Act 1889

s.25(1)

B in possession; sells to C (GF NN)

P4 Ltd

Merc A; in poss w/consent in ord course; B (GF WN)   Factors Act 1889, s.2

Hire-Purchase Act 1964 Part III;
Consumer Credit Act 1974 Schedule 4

s.21(2)(b)   Power of sale re-sale when orig B not paid

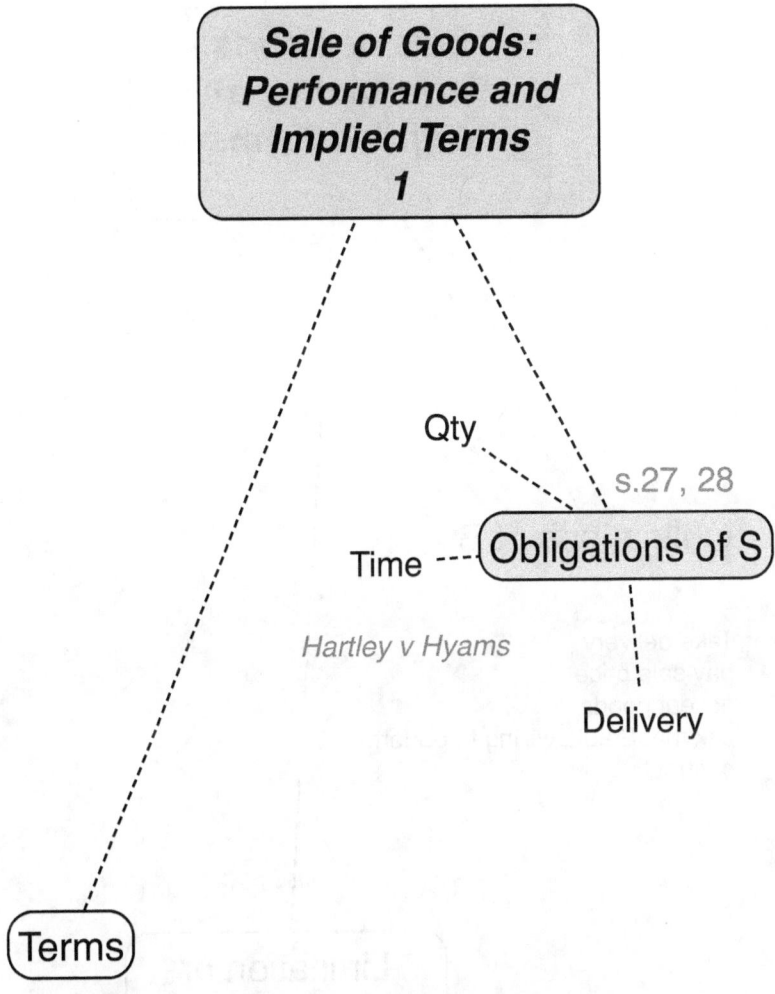

Sale of Goods: Performance and Implied Terms 1

Qty

s.27, 28

Time --- Obligations of S

Hartley v Hyams

Delivery

Terms

Conditions = entitled to discharge contract
Warranties = entitled to claim of damages
Innominate Terms = remedy depends on seriousness

Margaronis Navigation
Agency Ltd v Henry W
Peabody & Co Ltd

s.30

Sale of Goods: Performance and Implied Terms 2

Obligations of B

Take delivery
pay sale price
accept goods
ask that S able/willing to perform
contract

UCTA 1976   *Hong Kong Fir*

Limitation or Exclusion of Liability

caveat emptor; freedom of
conteact restricted by act
1. title/quiet possession, etc. (no)
2. Implied Ts (only when
reasonable)

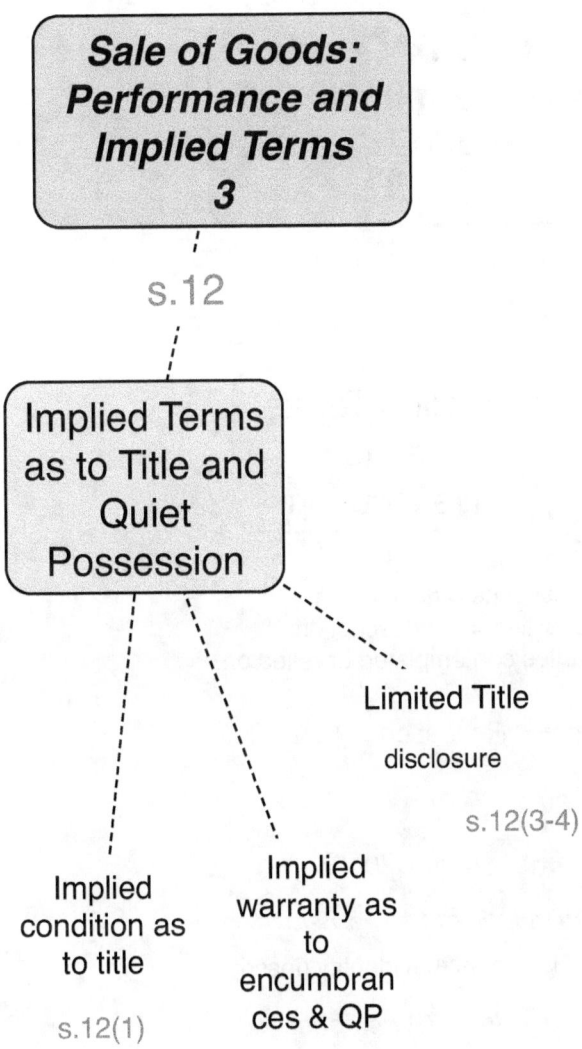

Sale of Goods: Performance and Implied Terms 3

s.12

Implied Terms as to Title and Quiet Possession

Limited Title

disclosure

s.12(3-4)

Implied condition as to title

s.12(1)

Implied warranty as to encumbrances & QP

Rowland v Divall

s.12(2) - damages only most covered by 12(1)

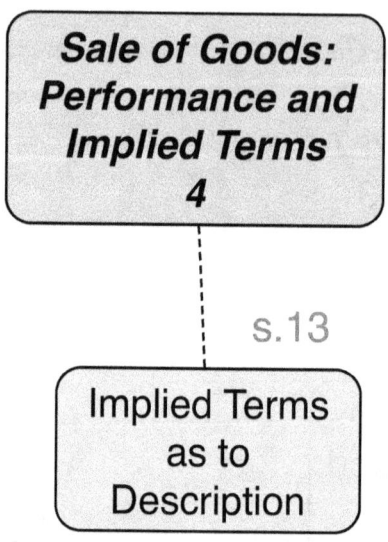

Sale of Goods: Performance and Implied Terms 4

s.13

Implied Terms as to Description

essence = description
qualities = not description
what parties contemplated or relied on

Arcos v Ronassen   *Re Moore*

strict
        Beale v Taylor   *Harlingdon*
comp.
        Brewer v Mann [2012]

Reardon Smith Lines Ltd v Hansen Tangen

means of ID, not actual identity description

Ashington Piggeries v Christopher Hill

'fair, average qual' not necessary to ID subject matter of contract

Chai Cher Watt v SDL Technologies Pte Ltd [2011]

Proton Energy Group SA v Orlen Lietuva [2013]

description is normally limited to the identification of the product

Sale of Goods: Performance and Implied Terms
5

exceptions to general rule of

caveat emptor

s.14(1)

apply to consumers and between merchants and agent course of business

Stevenson v Rogers

but

R & B Custom Brokers Co Ltd v United Dominions Trust Ltd

B did not disclose purpose, did not rely on S's skill.

Sale of Goods: Performance and Implied Terms
6

s.14(2)

in course of business

Implied Terms as to Satisfactory Quality

Bramhill v Edwards

reasonable person,
B with his
knowledge

Clegg v Andersson

added after much trying

Rogers v Parish (Scarborough) Ltd.

Lowe v W Machell Joinery Ltd [2011]

Richford v Parks of Hamilton (Townhead Garage) Ltd 2012

2d-hand goods

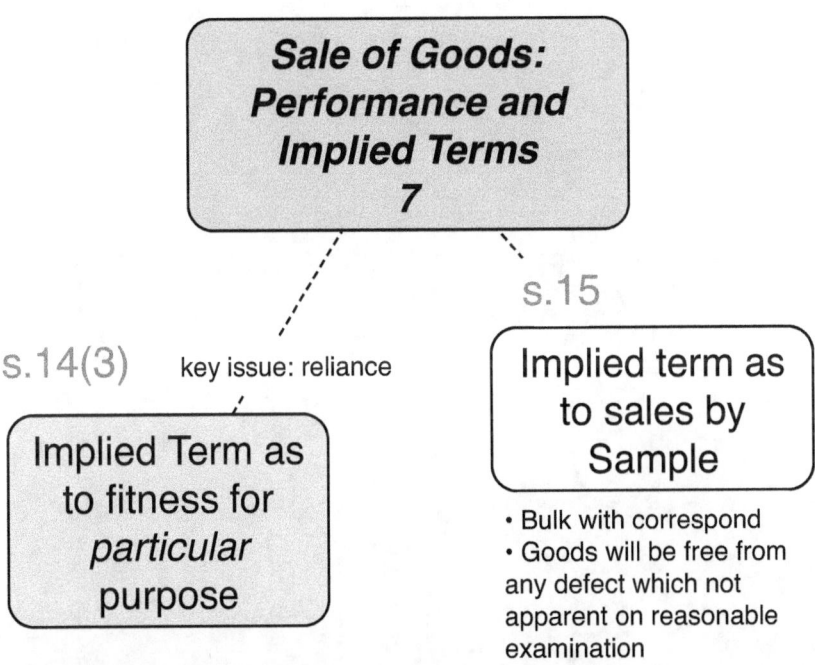

Sale of Goods: Performance and Implied Terms 7

s.14(3)   key issue: reliance

Implied Term as to fitness for *particular* purpose

s.15

Implied term as to sales by Sample

• Bulk with correspond
• Goods will be free from any defect which not apparent on reasonable examination

• in course of business; and
• B makes known purpose(s) (express or implied) OR it is reasonably foreseeable the purpose; and
• goods not reasonably fit

Griffiths v Peter Conway Ltd

Absolute obligation
Frost v Aylesbury Dairy

B must specify if unusual

Griffiths v Peter Conway

Henry Kendell & Sons v William Lillico & Sons
Trebor Bassett [2011]

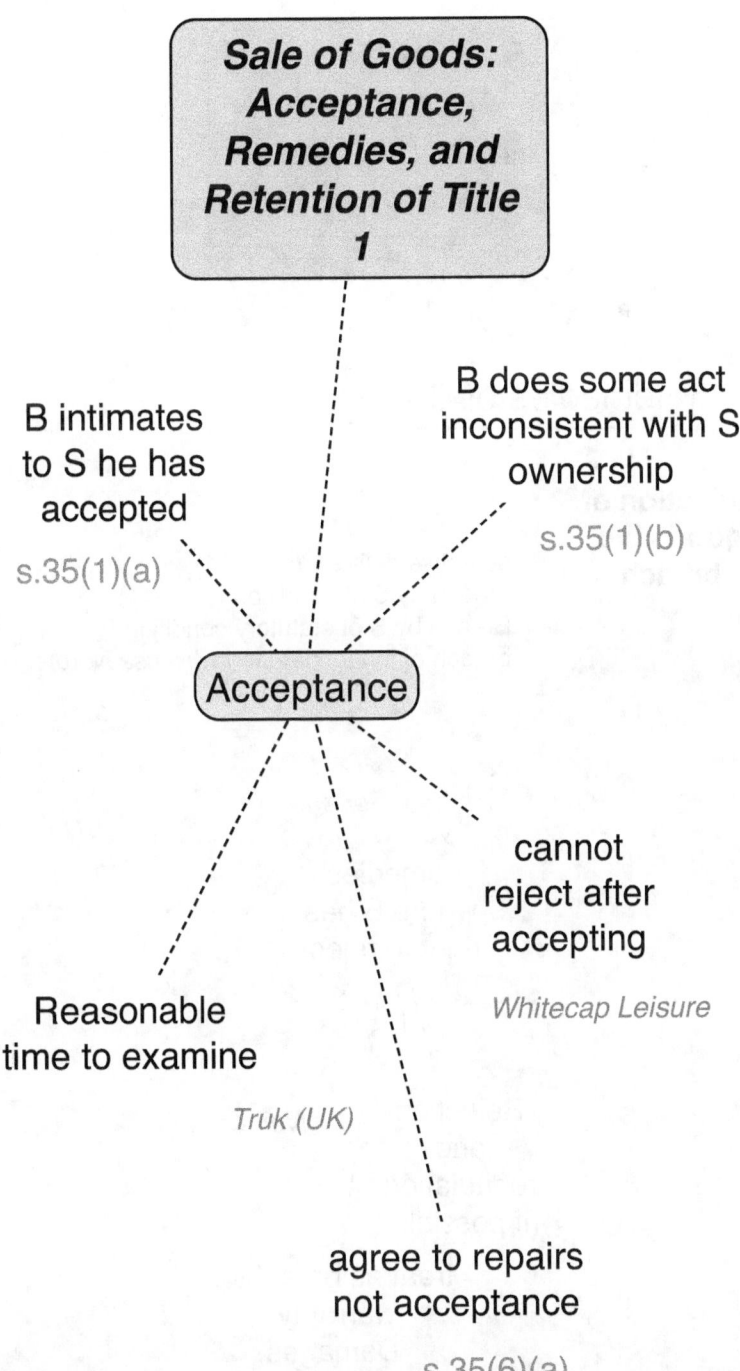

Sale of Goods: Acceptance, Remedies, and Retention of Title 1

B intimates to S he has accepted

s.35(1)(a)

B does some act inconsistent with S ownership

s.35(1)(b)

Acceptance

cannot reject after accepting

Whitecap Leisure

Reasonable time to examine

Truk (UK)

agree to repairs not acceptance

s.35(6)(a)

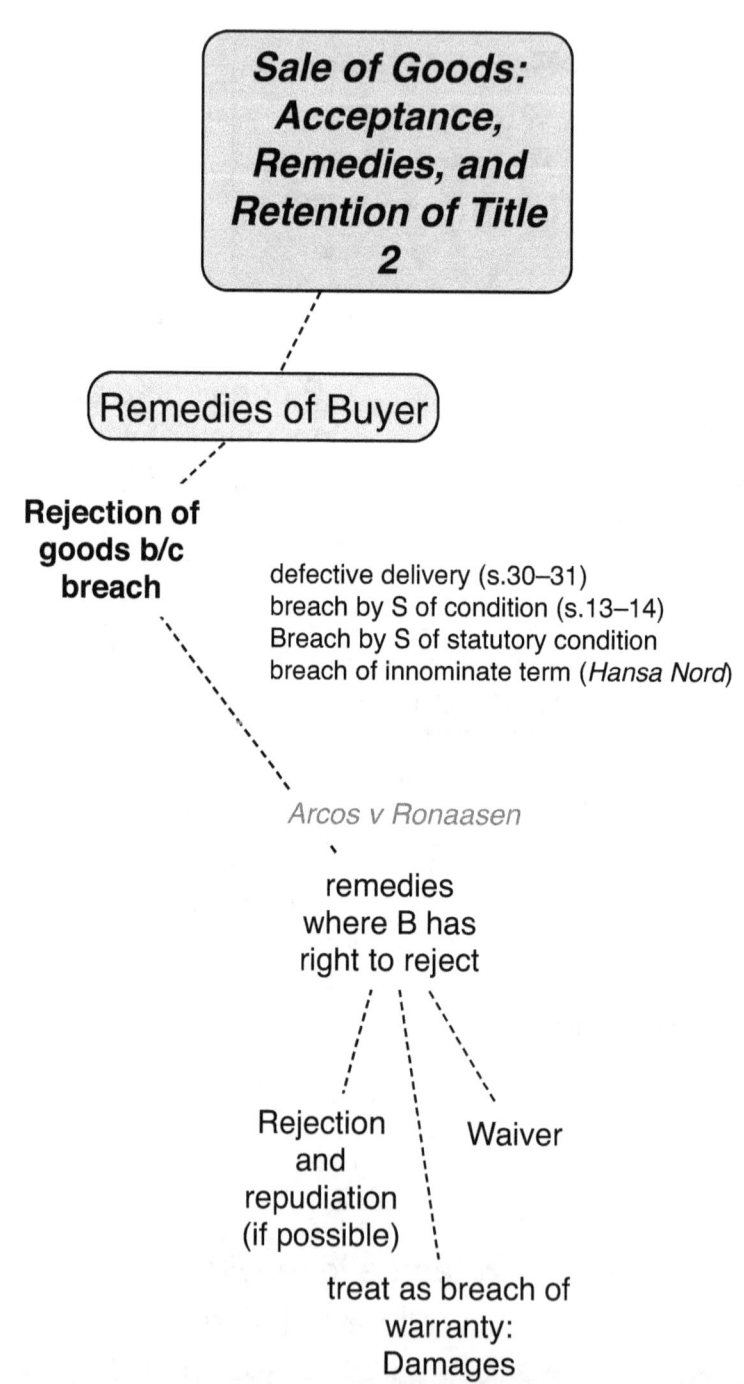

Sale of Goods: Acceptance, Remedies, and Retention of Title 2

Remedies of Buyer

Rejection of goods b/c breach

defective delivery (s.30–31)
breach by S of condition (s.13–14)
Breach by S of statutory condition
breach of innominate term (*Hansa Nord*)

Arcos v Ronaasen

remedies where B has right to reject

Rejection and repudiation (if possible)

Waiver

treat as breach of warranty: Damages

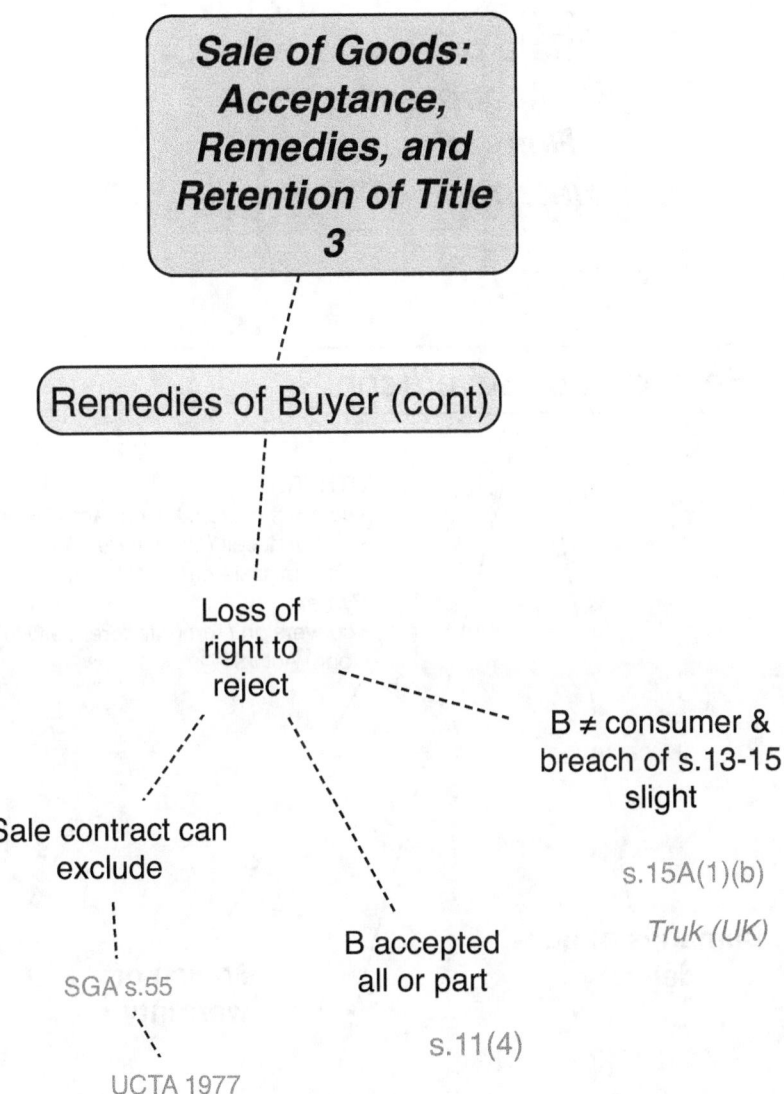

Sale of Goods: Acceptance, Remedies, and Retention of Title 3

Remedies of Buyer (cont)

Loss of right to reject

Sale contract can exclude

SGA s.55

UCTA 1977

B accepted all or part

s.11(4)

B ≠ consumer & breach of s.13-15 slight

s.15A(1)(b)

Truk (UK)

30

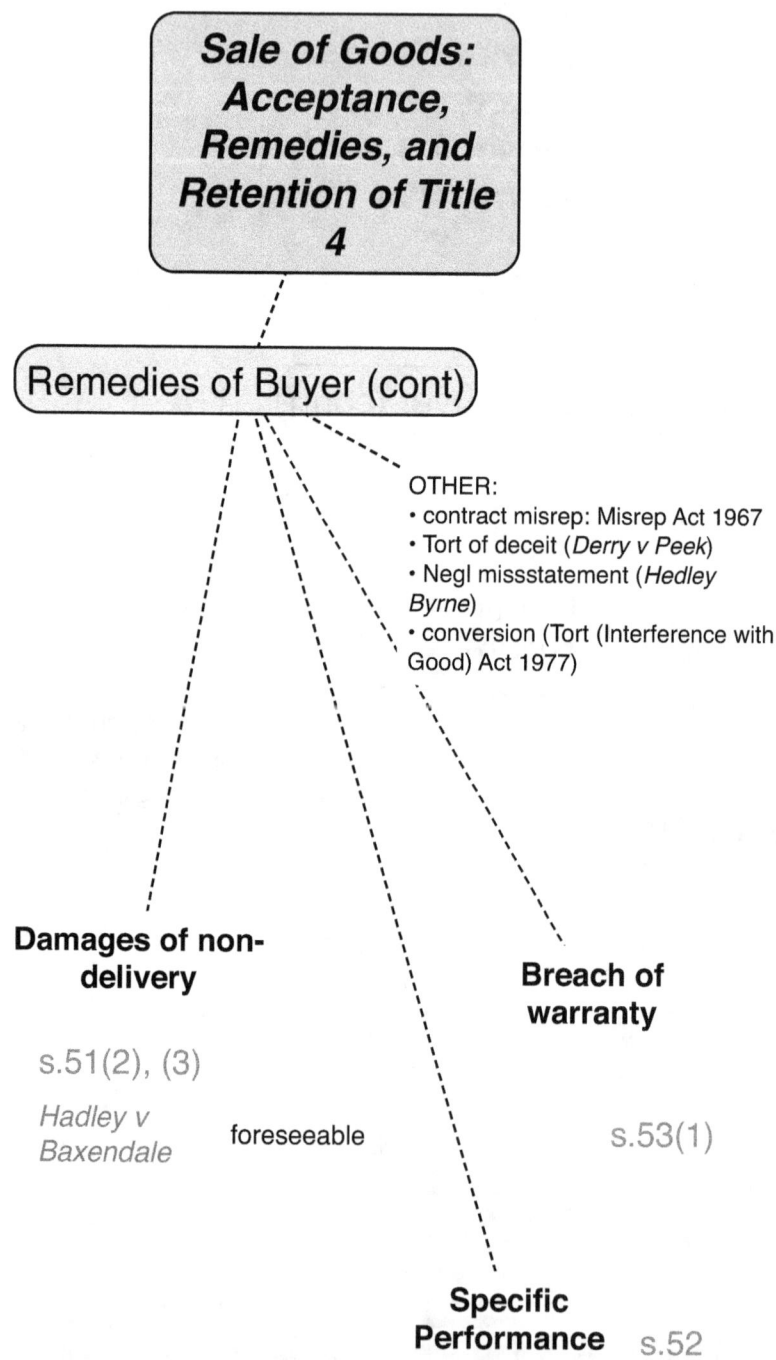

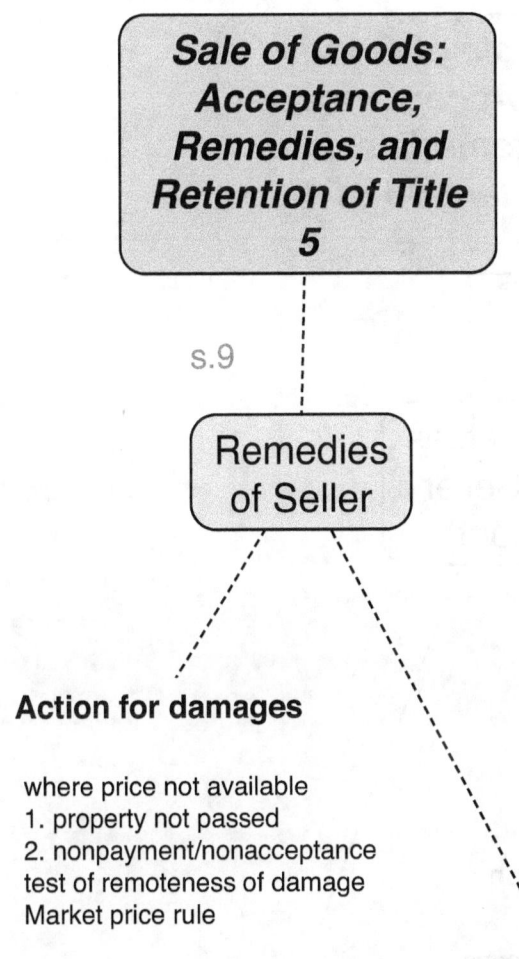

Sale of Goods: Acceptance, Remedies, and Retention of Title 5

s.9

Remedies of Seller

Action for damages

where price not available
1. property not passed
2. nonpayment/nonacceptance
test of remoteness of damage
Market price rule

Action for the Price

certainty, preciseness
only where
1. where contract
2. risk has passed before property
3. property passed to B

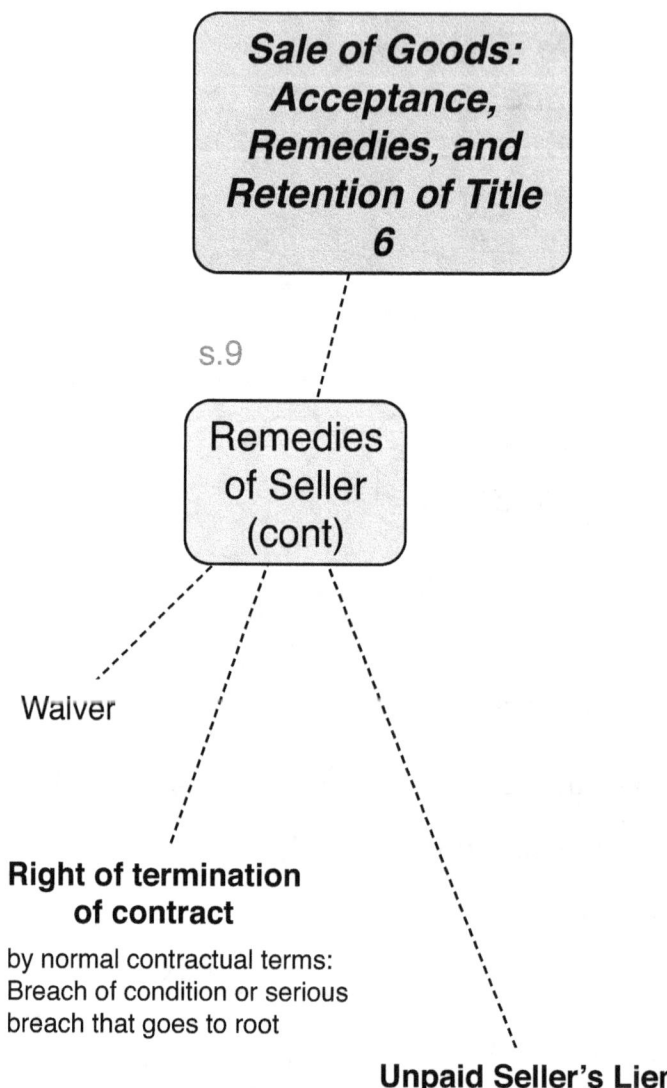

Sale of Goods: Acceptance, Remedies, and Retention of Title 6

s.9

Remedies of Seller (cont)

Waiver

Right of termination of contract

by normal contractual terms: Breach of condition or serious breach that goes to root

Unpaid Seller's Lien

exercised in rem
1. lein-possessory security
2. s.44-46 B insolvent (right of stoppage in transit
3. Right of resale

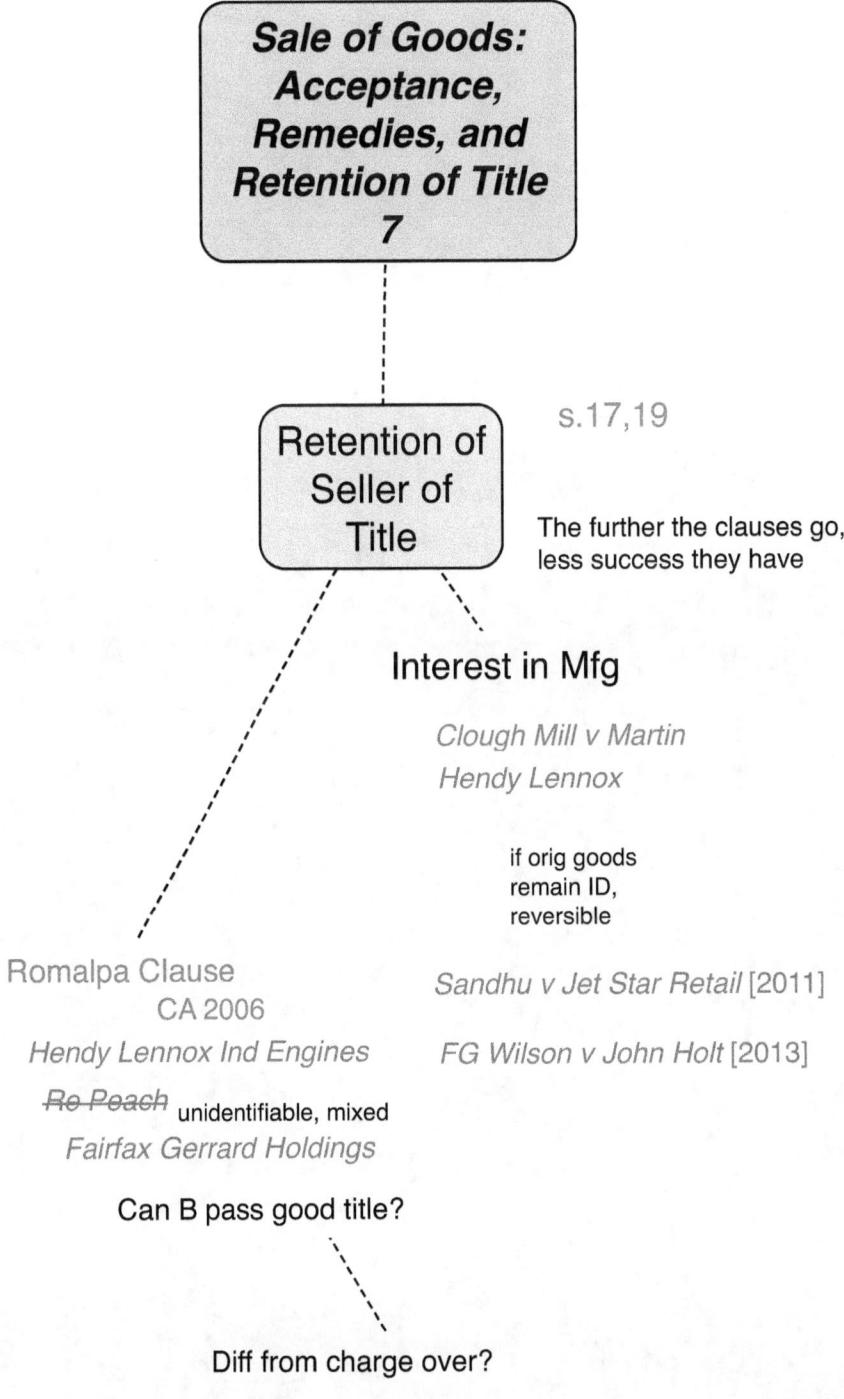

Sale of Goods: Acceptance, Remedies, and Retention of Title

7

Retention of Seller of Title

s.17,19

The further the clauses go, less success they have

Interest in Mfg

Clough Mill v Martin
Hendy Lennox

if orig goods remain ID, reversible

Romalpa Clause
CA 2006
Hendy Lennox Ind Engines
~~Re Peach~~ unidentifiable, mixed
Fairfax Gerrard Holdings

Sandhu v Jet Star Retail [2011]

FG Wilson v John Holt [2013]

Can B pass good title?

Diff from charge over?

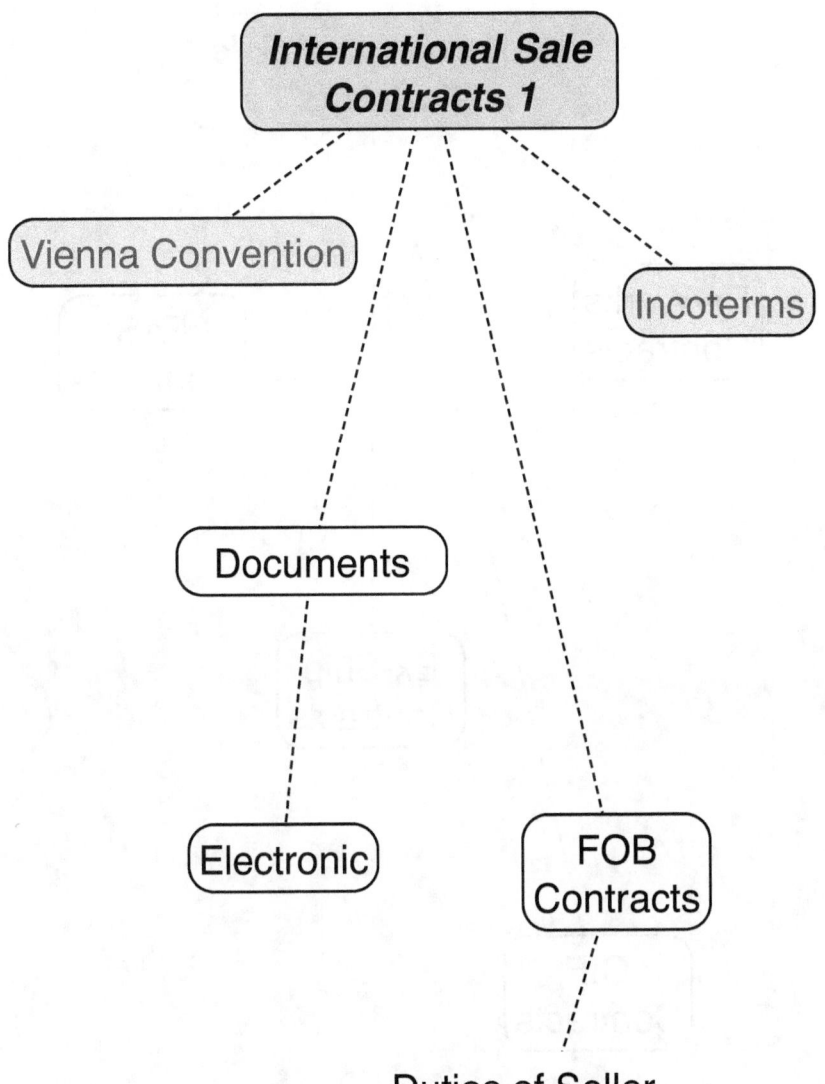

International Sale Contracts 1

Vienna Convention

Incoterms

Documents

Electronic

FOB Contracts

Duties of Seller
Duties of Buyer
Transfer of PRoperty and Risk
Remedies for Seller
Remedies for Buyer

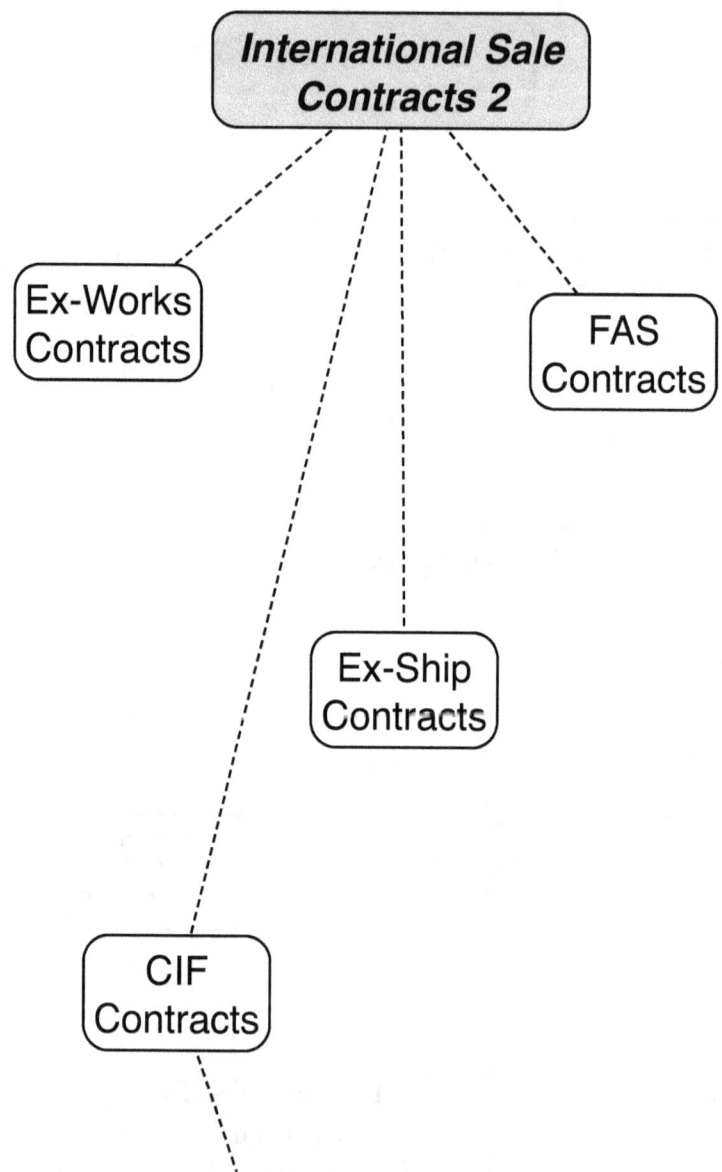

Duties of Seller (goods, docs)
Duties of Buyer
Transfer of Property and Risk

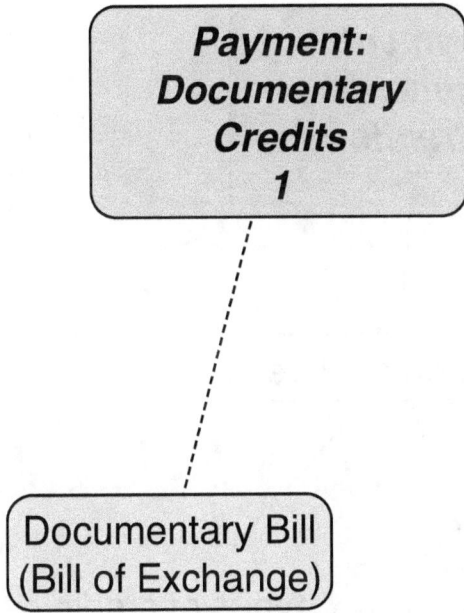

**Unconditional order in writing
Negotiable
Without assignment
Transferee acquires full rights**

**Problems: failure to pay,
conversaion, Negotiable
Without assignment
Transferee acquires full rights**

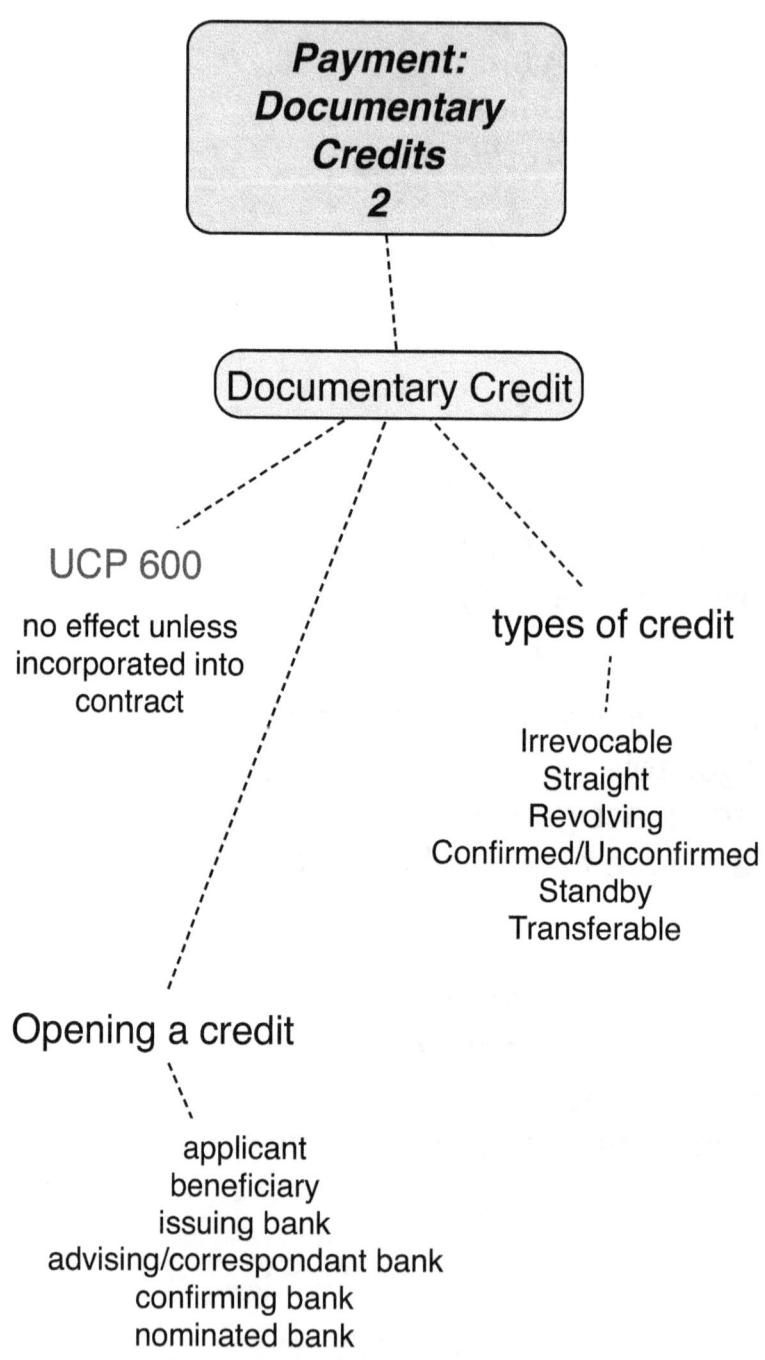

Payment: Documentary Credits 2

Documentary Credit

UCP 600

no effect unless incorporated into contract

types of credit

Irrevocable
Straight
Revolving
Confirmed/Unconfirmed
Standby
Transferable

Opening a credit

applicant
beneficiary
issuing bank
advising/correspondant bank
confirming bank
nominated bank

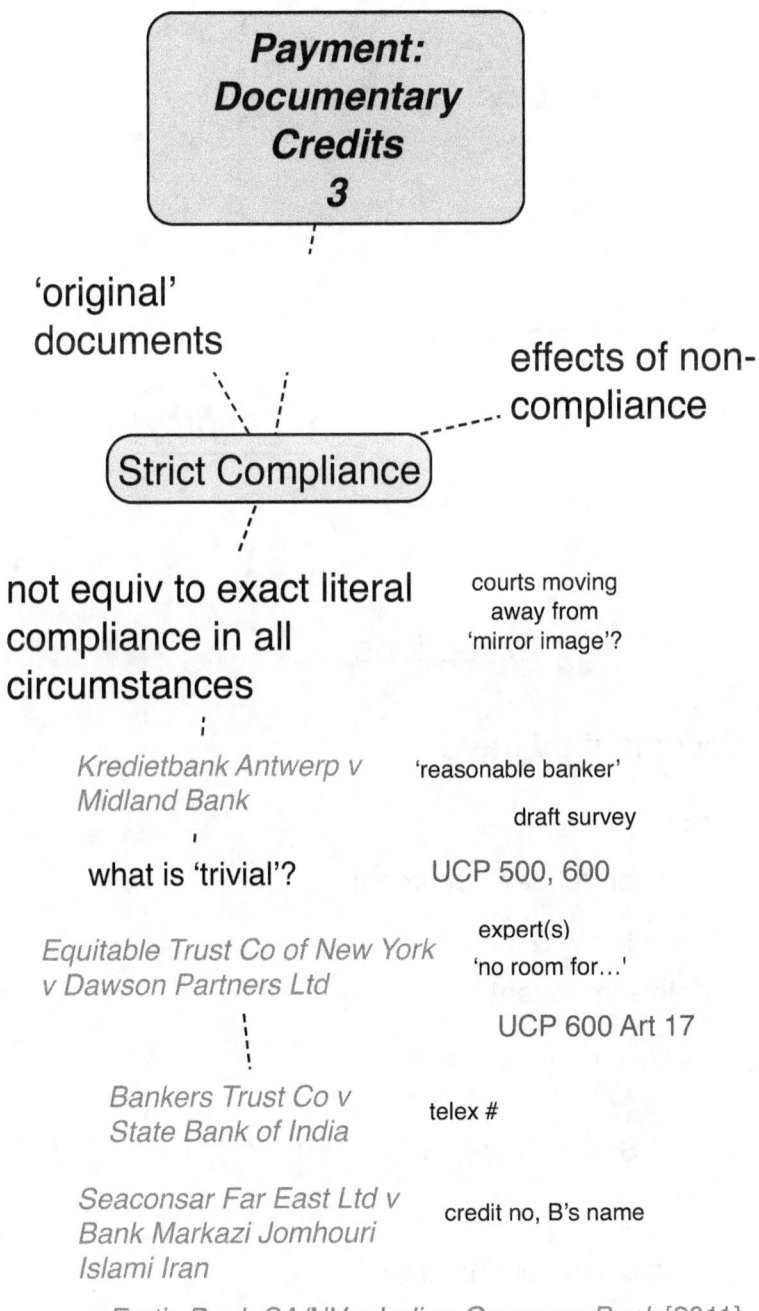

Payment: Documentary Credits 3

'original' documents

effects of non-compliance

Strict Compliance

not equiv to exact literal compliance in all circumstances

courts moving away from 'mirror image'?

Kredietbank Antwerp v Midland Bank

'reasonable banker'

draft survey

what is 'trivial'?

UCP 500, 600

Equitable Trust Co of New York v Dawson Partners Ltd

expert(s)
'no room for...'

UCP 600 Art 17

Bankers Trust Co v State Bank of India

telex #

Seaconsar Far East Ltd v Bank Markazi Jomhouri Islami Iran

credit no, B's name

Fortis Bank SA/NV v Indian Overseas Bank [2011]

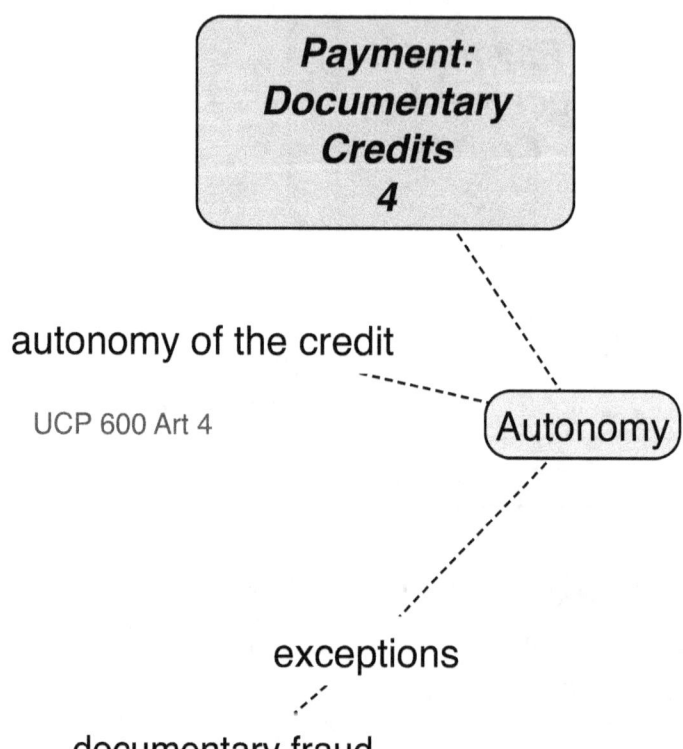

Payment: Documentary Credits 4

autonomy of the credit

UCP 600 Art 4

Autonomy

exceptions

documentary fraud

~~UCP 600~~

on face of document

S or A know & intend

Motive irrelevant

Standard Chartered Bank v Pakistan National Shipping Corp (no. 2)

S/A unaware, GF

The American Accord

compelling but not irrefutable

Society of Lloyd's v Canadian Imperial Bank of Canada

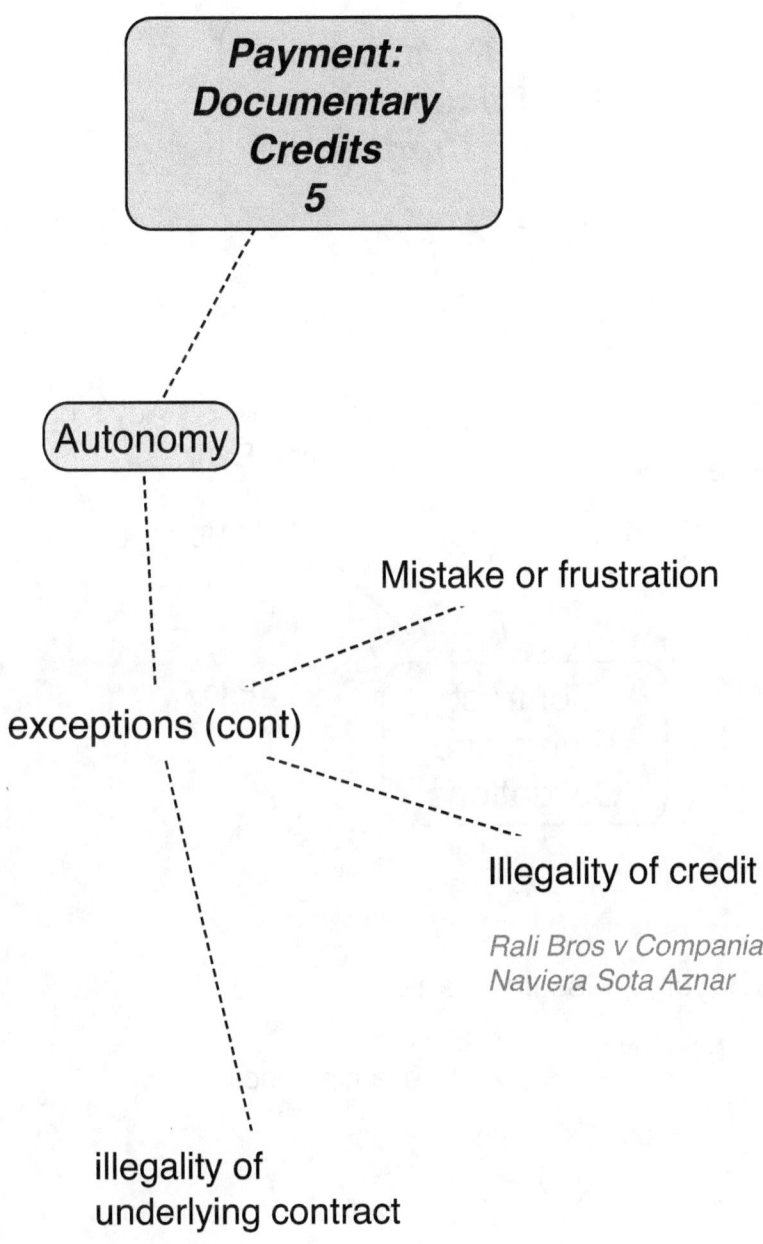

**Payment:
Documentary
Credits
5**

Autonomy

Mistake or frustration

exceptions (cont)

Illegality of credit

*Rali Bros v Compania
Naviera Sota Aznar*

illegality of
underlying contract

*Group Jose Re v
Walbrook Insurance Co
Ltd*

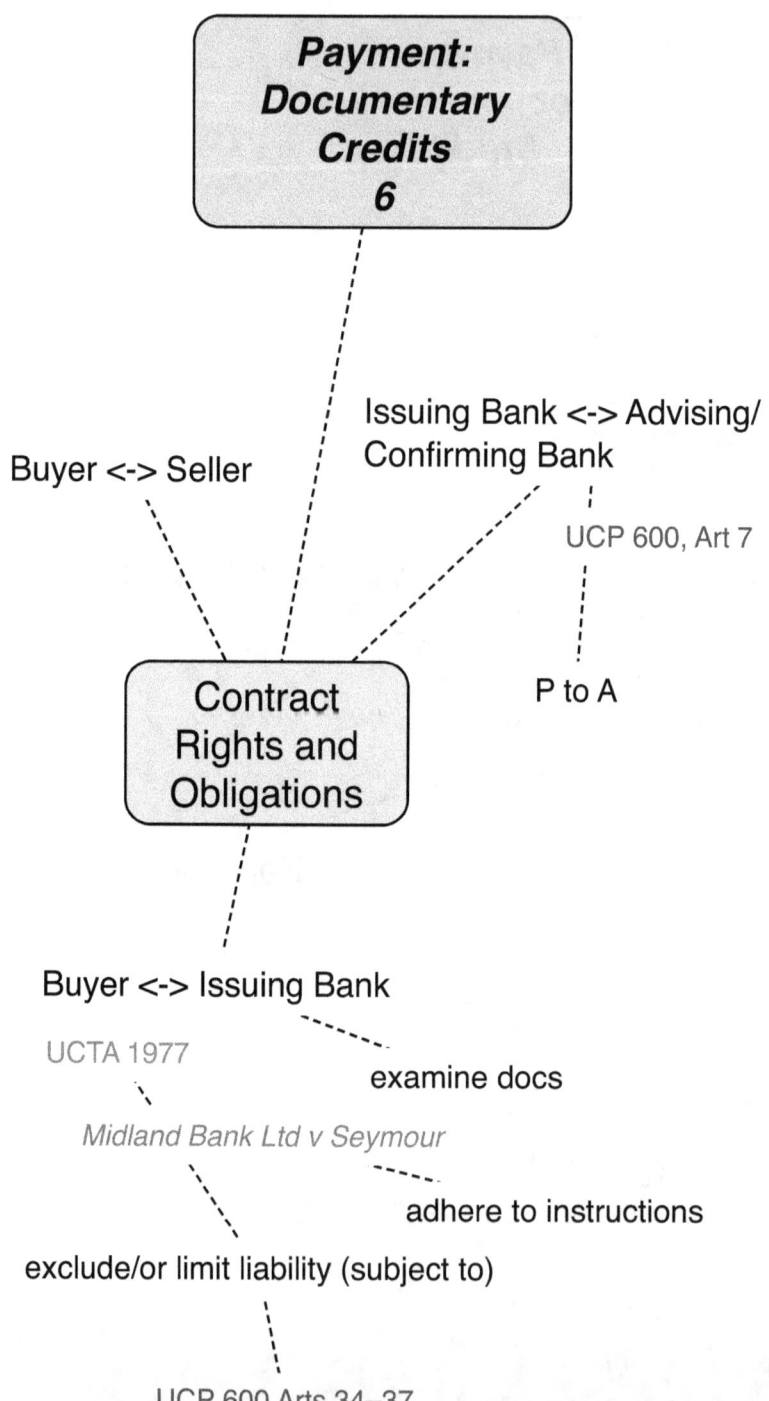

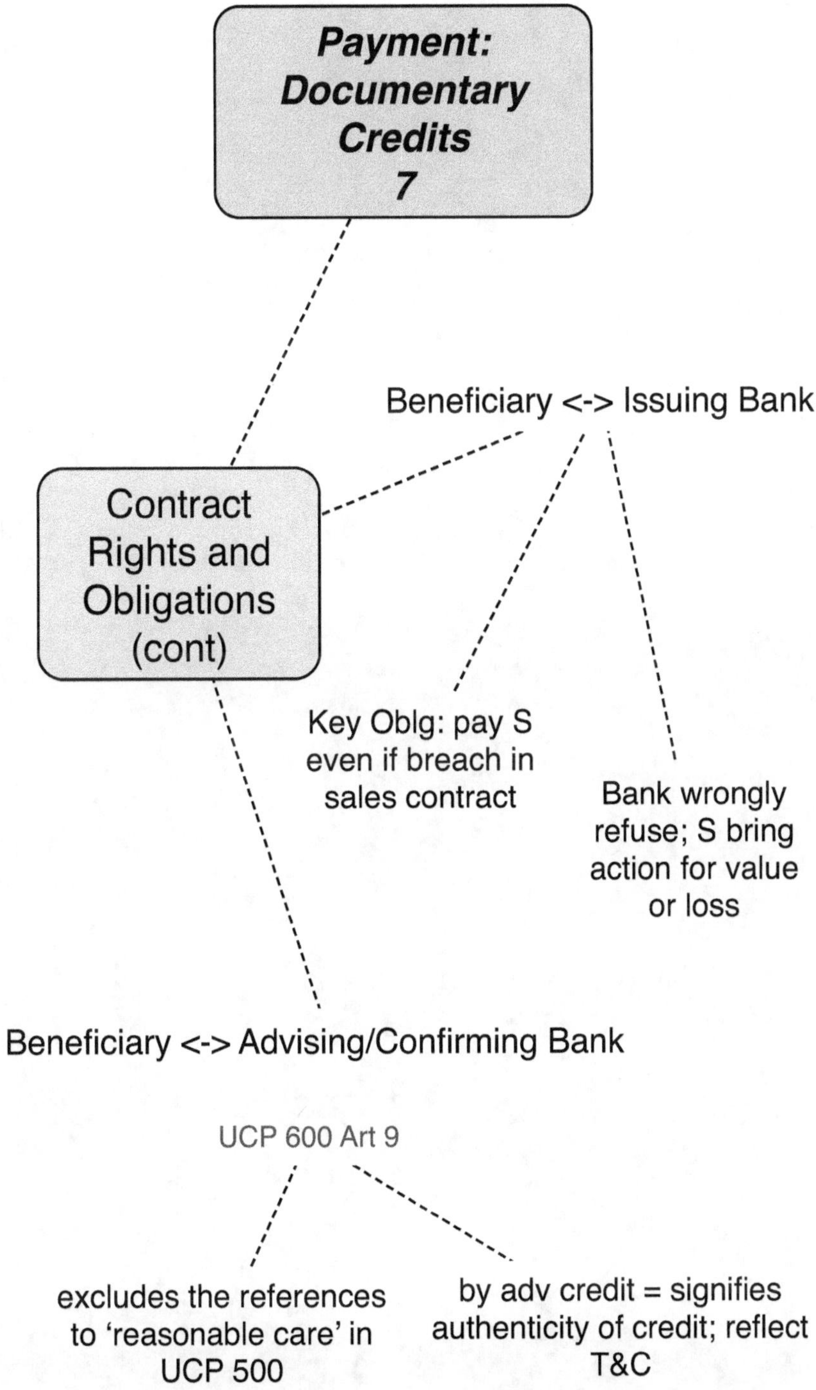

Payment:
**Documentary
Credits
7**

Beneficiary <-> Issuing Bank

Contract
Rights and
Obligations
(cont)

Key Oblg: pay S
even if breach in
sales contract

Bank wrongly
refuse; S bring
action for value
or loss

Beneficiary <-> Advising/Confirming Bank

UCP 600 Art 9

excludes the references
to 'reasonable care' in
UCP 500

by adv credit = signifies
authenticity of credit; reflect
T&C

ABOUT THE AUTHOR

Dr. Markus McDowell holds a law degree from the University of London. As a teacher, writer, and law clerk, he has researched and taught extensively about learning methods and techniques. He is the Editor-in-Chief of *Legal Issues Journal*.

www.ingramcontent.com/pod-product-compliance
Lightning Source LLC
Chambersburg PA
CBHW070411190526
45169CB00003B/1213